Especially for

....

From

....

Date

....

WONDERFUL
NAMES OF
JESUS

WONDERFUL NAMES OF JESUS

52 Devotions for Kids

MariLee Parrish

BARBOUR **kidz**
A Division of Barbour Publishing

CONTENTS

Did you know that the name of Jesus is very powerful? Some of the most powerful prayers are simply: "Jesus!" In those moments you are declaring the power of Jesus and asking for His help and protection. Philippians 2:10 (NLT) tells us that "at the name of Jesus every knee should bow, in heaven and on earth and under the earth."

You have power in the name of Jesus to get rid of any evil you come up against. Wow! How do we know that's really true? James 4:7 (AMP) says, "Submit to [the authority of] God. Resist the devil [stand firm against him] and he will flee from you."

Is there some fear you're dealing with? Call on the name of Jesus for help. Are you in need of Jesus to come and rescue you in some way? Say His name!

In the pages of this book, we are going to go through scripture and learn about the many names of Jesus and why knowing these names is important for us as children of God.

Thank You, Jesus, for Your powerful name!

A STAR

"I see Him, but not now;
I behold Him, but not near;
a Star shall come out of Jacob."

NUMBERS 24:17 NKJV

What first comes to mind when you think of a "star"? Do you think of the five-pointed object you learned to draw in kindergarten? Do you think of twinkly lights in the night sky? Or do you think of famous kids on YouTube?

One of the names of Jesus is Star. The original meaning of this word could refer to a star, a prince, a ruler, a light. Jesus is all of those things to us. Numbers 24:17 is a prophecy about the coming Savior.

In Bible times, the study of the stars and the sky was very important. The Magi saw a new star when Jesus was born, and that star guided them all the way to the newborn King. We don't know a lot about the Magi, also known as the wise men, but they are thought to have been astrologers who studied the night sky and knew ancient documents. They likely knew of the prophecy told in the book of Numbers about the coming star—the long-awaited Savior.

The Magi followed the star for thousands of miles so that they could worship this tiny King who would one day save the whole world. How about you? Do you worship Jesus too?

It's easy to make TV stars, video games, and being liked really important in our lives. But Jesus is the real Star who deserves all of our love and admiration. Will you give Him all of your devotion like the wise men did?

Jesus, I'm so thankful You came for me.
You showed up as a little baby but grew up to save
me from all of my sins. I invite You into my heart,
and I want to make You the center of my life.
You are the Star I want to follow my whole life.

THINK ABOUT IT:

How is Jesus a star to you? What can you do to make Him the focus of your heart?

THE LIGHT
OF THE MORNING

"He shines on them like the morning light.
He is like the sunshine on a morning without
clouds. He is like rain that makes the
new grass grow out of the earth
through sunshine after rain."

2 Samuel 23:4 NLV

Have you ever been afraid of the dark? It's okay. A lot of people are—even grown-ups! Jesus wants us to take those fears straight to Him. Why? Because Jesus is the light of the whole world.

John 1:4–5 (NIV) says, "In him was life, and that life was the light of all mankind. The light shines in the darkness, and the darkness has not overcome it." This verse is not just talking about the lack of daylight; it's talking about a darkness of evil and bad things.

The Bible is a book we can trust because it is the written Word of God. And speaking of light, Psalm 119:105 (NIV) says, "Your word is a lamp for my feet, a light on my path." The Bible is like a flashlight to help us see in a dark world.

The Bible, also known as God's Word, tells us that darkness and evil will never overpower the light of Jesus! So anytime you're afraid of the dark—whether it's after your lights go out in your room or it's a fear of evil—you can remember that the light of Jesus shines brightly in you. If you've asked Jesus to come into your heart, then you can be sure this is true. The Bible promises that the darkness will never be more powerful than the light that is alive inside of you because of Jesus! Now, how amazing is that?

Another thing to remember is the simple prayer you can pray when you're afraid of the dark: "Jesus!" That's it! Say His name in faithful prayer and trust that His light is with you, making darkness disappear.

Jesus, thank You for being my light
and reminding me that You are more
powerful than any darkness I face.

THINK ABOUT IT:
When you think of Jesus and the Bible
as lights, how does that help you overcome
your fear of darkness and evil?

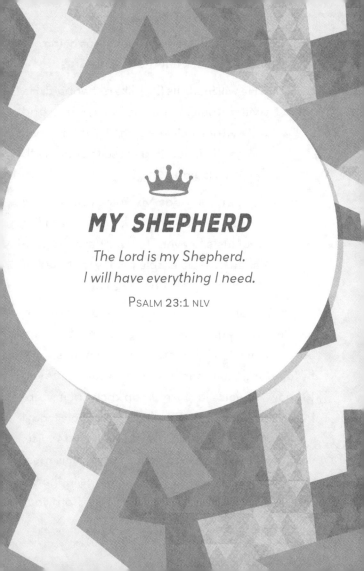

MY SHEPHERD

The Lord is my Shepherd.
I will have everything I need.

Psalm 23:1 NLV

The Bible has a lot to say about Jesus being our Shepherd. Check out these scriptures:

▶ "He will feed His flock like a shepherd. He will gather the lambs in His arms and carry them close to His heart. He will be gentle in leading those that are with young" (Isaiah 40:11 NLV).

▶ "My sheep hear My voice and I know them. They follow Me. I give them life that lasts forever. They will never be punished. No one is able to take them out of My hand" (John 10:27–28 NLV).

In sheepherding countries, sheep from different flocks may get together to graze, but they can easily be divided back into their own herd simply by following their master's voice. Jesus wants you to know His voice just like sheep know their shepherd's voice. Yep, God still talks to His people today!

As you begin learning how to hear God's voice, you'll see that when God speaks to you, His message will always line up with His words in the Bible. If you are not sure if something is from your imagination or from God, simply ask God to be clear to you.

Usually, if there is something God really wants you to do or to know, you will hear it again and again—through His Word, through a song, through a pastor or teacher at church. God can speak to us in so many ways. . .if we're listening!

Decide today that you are going to stay close to your Shepherd, Jesus. He will always lead you on the right path. He will give you everything you need. Pray that Jesus continues to make His voice known to you.

Jesus, thank You for caring for me like a gentle shepherd. I will follow You, Jesus. Help me to recognize You as You speak to me. Please open my ears to get to know Your voice. I want to follow You with all of my heart.

THINK ABOUT IT:
Jesus is your gentle Shepherd. Can you picture Him carrying you close to His heart?

THE STRONG AND MIGHTY LORD

Who is this King of glory?
The Lord strong and mighty,
the Lord mighty in battle.

Psalm 24:8 KJV

Our God is a mighty God. He is the High King and more powerful than anything else in all of the universe. And at the same time, He loves and cares about you as His precious child. He is a mighty king and a loving father. Zephaniah 3:16–17 (NLT) makes this very clear: "Cheer up, Zion! Don't be afraid! For the LORD your God is living among you. He is a mighty savior. He will take delight in you with gladness. With his love, he will calm all your fears. He will rejoice over you with joyful songs." In this verse, "Zion" could refer to "God's people"—and that includes you! So cheer up, God's people. Your God is strong and loving. He even sings over you. Wow! What an awesome God we have.

The book of Psalms in the Bible includes a bunch of poems that people would sing in Bible times. The psalms also tell of the greatness of God. Here's a good one: "Great is our [majestic and mighty] Lord and abundant in strength; His understanding is inexhaustible [infinite, boundless]" (Psalm 147:5 AMP).

These verses tell us the truth of who God is

and what He is like. He knows more than anyone on earth, even the smartest person alive! God is the Creator of all things. Now let this one blow your mind: God even created *time*! How is that even possible? The Bible also tells us that what is impossible with man is possible with God (Luke 18:27)—that's how!

So if you are ever feeling alone, or scared, or worried about the future, remember that the mighty God of the Bible is the same God who is alive in you at this very moment. He is able to fight for you and take care of any of your problems. He is mighty and He is good.

Thank You, Jesus, for taking care of me.
Help me not to worry but to remember that
You are bigger than anything I face.

THINK ABOUT IT:
How do you need Jesus to
be mighty for you today?

EXCELLENT

Let them praise the name of the Lord:
for his name alone is excellent; his glory
is above the earth and heaven.

PSALM 148:13 KJV

Has anyone ever told you that your work was excellent? Maybe a picture you drew or some sort of masterpiece you created? Or maybe you got a perfect score on a test and your teacher told you it was excellent. *Excellent* means really, really, really good. And guess what? That's one of the names of Jesus. He is excellent. He is really, really, really good!

Do you know what a character trait is? It's something in your personality that probably won't change as you grow up. It's one of the things that makes you, you. For example, *loyal* and *adventurous* are examples of character traits. One of the character traits of Jesus is that He is really, really, really good—He's excellent! The goodness and beauty of Jesus will never change. His heart is good, and He always wants what is good for you too.

Jesus is the most excellent over all creation. A lot of things that God made are pretty excellent too. Have you ever seen the mountains in person? Or the ocean? Rainbows and trees and animals are amazing too. The beauty of God's creation helps us remember how excellent God is.

Did you know that God asks us to think about excellent things? Look what these verses say: "Finally, brothers and sisters, whatever is true, whatever is noble, whatever is right, whatever is pure, whatever is lovely, whatever is admirable—if anything is excellent or praiseworthy—think about such things. Whatever you have learned or received or heard from me, or seen in me—put it into practice. And the God of peace will be with you" (Philippians 4:8–9 NIV).

When you are having a hard time with your attitude, take a look at your thoughts. The things we think about usually become the things we do. The Holy Spirit inside you can help you flip the switch from thinking about negative things to thinking about things that are excellent.

Jesus, please help me switch my thoughts from negative to excellent!

THINK ABOUT IT:
What we think about is very important to Jesus! How can you train your mind to think about excellent things?

A FRIEND WHO STAYS NEARER THAN A BROTHER

A man who has friends must be a friend, but there is a friend who stays nearer than a brother.

PROVERBS 18:24 NLV

Because of all that Jesus did for us on the cross, He made us children of God! But we're not just His children; He actually calls us His friends! John 15:14–15 (NLV) says, "You are My friends if you do what I tell you. I do not call you servants that I own anymore. A servant does not know what his owner is doing. I call you friends, because I have told you everything I have heard from My Father."

Have you ever thought about what being a friend of Jesus means? When you look for a friend, you want someone who is kind, trustworthy, and willing to listen. Jesus is all of that and so much more. Imagine that the Creator and King of the world is your best friend! Now, believe it, because the Bible tells us it's true!

Jesus wants to have a close personal friendship with you. He wants you to know that you are never ever alone! And because of all that, you can live a life of confidence and joy, knowing that God is working everything out for your good and His glory—even the bad things that happen during this life (Romans 8:28).

Romans 5:2 (NLT) tells us, "Because of our faith,

Christ has brought us into this place of undeserved privilege where we now stand, and we confidently and joyfully look forward to sharing God's glory." Being friends with Jesus is one of our "undeserved privileges." Jesus gave His life for us so that we could be friends with Him now and for all eternity.

Take some time to write Jesus a note, just like you would your best friend. Tell Him how it makes you feel to know He wants to be your best friend. You can tell Him anything, and He will always welcome you into His heart.

*Jesus, how awesome that You call me
Your friend! That makes me confident that
I can go through life with joy in my heart!*

THINK ABOUT IT:
What can you do this week to get
to know your Friend Jesus better?

WONDERFUL COUNSELOR

For to us a Child is born, to us a son is given,
and the government will be on his shoulders.
And he will be called Wonderful Counselor,
Mighty God, Everlasting Father,
Prince of Peace.

Isaiah 9:6 NIV

The names of Jesus help us to know what kind of God we serve. His name is powerful, and He offers everything your heart needs. Isaiah tells us that He is called the "Wonderful Counselor" (9:6 NIV). Jesus holds all the wisdom and knowledge we could ever need.

In Colossians 2:2–3 (NLT) the apostle Paul writes, "I want them to be encouraged and knit together by strong ties of love. I want them to have complete confidence that they understand God's mysterious plan, which is Christ himself. In him lie hidden all the treasures of wisdom and knowledge."

Jesus has the perfect answer to every one of your questions. God wants us to understand who He is. He wants us to know what His names mean so that we seek Him for every little detail of our lives. Nothing is too small or too big to take to God. He wants you to come to Him for everything. How wonderful!

The Bible reminds us again and again how wonderful God is. Here are a few verses that help us remember:

- "Let them give thanks to the LORD for his unfailing love and his wonderful deeds for mankind" (Psalm 107:21 NIV).

- "Help me understand the meaning of your commandments, and I will meditate on your wonderful deeds" (Psalm 119:27 NLT).

- "All this also comes from the LORD Almighty, whose plan is wonderful, whose wisdom is magnificent" (Isaiah 28:29 NIV).

Pick your favorite out of those scriptures and write it on a sticky note. Post it on your wall so you can remember how wonderful God is every day.

Your names mean so much to me, Jesus.
I praise You for being my Wonderful Counselor,
my Mighty God, my Everlasting Father, and my
Prince of Peace. You've made a way to take care
of every need I have. You are wonderful!

THINK ABOUT IT:
How have you seen the wonder
of God during your lifetime?

THE EVERLASTING FATHER

For unto us a child is born, unto us a son is given: and the government shall be upon his shoulder: and his name shall be called Wonderful, Counsellor, The mighty God, The everlasting Father, The Prince of Peace.

Isaiah 9:6 KJV

Jesus has a special place in His heart for kids. Kids have always been very important to Him. Look at this verse: "Jesus said, 'Let the little children come to me. Don't stop them, because the kingdom of heaven belongs to people who are like these children' " (Matthew 19:14 ICB).

The disciples were actually scolding the parents for letting their kids bother Jesus. But Jesus scolded the disciples instead. He wanted the kids to come to Him. Jesus loves kids so much. The Bible says that Jesus is our Everlasting Father. As Jesus welcomed the little children in His lap, so He welcomes you.

Matthew 18:2–5 (NLT) shows us another time that Jesus welcomed children: "Jesus called a little child to him and put the child among them. Then he said, 'I tell you the truth, unless you turn from your sins and become like little children, you will never get into the Kingdom of Heaven. So anyone who becomes as humble as this little child is the greatest in the Kingdom of Heaven. And anyone who welcomes a little child like this on my behalf is welcoming me.' "

See how important you are to Jesus? Some kids grow up without a dad or without a good one or with a dad who is too busy for the little details of his kids' lives. That can be very hard and sad. Or maybe you have a great relationship with your earthly father, and that is something to be extra thankful for. No matter what kind of relationship you have with your earthly father, Jesus wants to be your heavenly Father now and forever. No dad is perfect except for your heavenly Father! Allow Jesus to meet the "father" needs in your heart. He can fill the empty spaces that no earthly father ever could.

Jesus, thank You for welcoming me
and loving me so well! I'm glad
You're my heavenly Dad forever.

THINK ABOUT IT:
Can you picture yourself climbing onto
Jesus' lap and letting Him love you
like a good and perfect father?

THE PRINCE OF PEACE

For to us a Child will be born. To us a Son will be given. And the rule of the nations will be on His shoulders. His name will be called Wonderful, Teacher, Powerful God, Father Who Lives Forever, Prince of Peace.

Isaiah 9:6 NLV

Have you ever been really worried about something? Maybe a test at school or going to get a shot? It's easy to make yourself nervous about something. Jesus cares about you so much that He tells you not to worry. "Do not worry about tomorrow. Tomorrow will have its own worries. The troubles we have in a day are enough for one day" (Matthew 6:34 NLV).

Why does Jesus say this? One of the reasons is because worrying is actually bad for your body. Worrying can cause your body to release stress hormones that make your heart work harder, it can cause you to feel tired and grumpy, and it can even slow down your body's ability to fight disease. So Jesus tells us simply not to do it! He wants you to have His peace even in the midst of scary situations.

Jesus is our Prince of Peace. Philippians 4:7 (NLV) tells us a little more about God's peace: "The peace of God is much greater than the human mind can understand. This peace will keep your hearts and minds through Christ Jesus."

Peace is also one of the fruits of the Spirit listed

in Galatians 5:22–23. The fruit of peace is a supernatural ability to stay calm in the middle of anything. In fact, God's peace in the middle of problems is beyond what any human can understand. God Himself has to grow this special fruit in your heart.

God asks us to replace all of our worries with prayer. So when you're feeling crummy about something, instead of complaining or being afraid, talk to God. Tell Him what's on your mind, and thank Him for what He has done and what He will do. That's when God supernaturally changes your worries into a true and lasting peace.

Jesus, I know You are strong enough to handle all of my worries. I bring all of them to You and ask You to replace them with the peace that comes from trusting You.

THINK ABOUT IT:
What worry do you need Jesus
to replace with His peace?

A SHADOW FROM THE HEAT

For You have been a strong-place for those who could not help themselves and for those in need because of much trouble. You have been a safe place from the storm and a shadow from the heat. For the breath of the one who shows no pity is like a storm against a wall.

ISAIAH 25:4 NLV

*T*oday's verse tells us that Jesus is a shadow from the heat! What does that mean? It's like shade on a hot summer day. Have you ever spent the day swimming in the sunshine? Unless you take a break in the shade and wear a lot of sunscreen, you might get a nasty sunburn. Or maybe you're playing outside in the summer heat and you start getting really hot and sweaty. What do you need? Some shade! The best parks and pools have trees and shade available. A good shade tree or umbrella helps protect us from the strong power of the sun. Jesus protects us like that too.

The Message paraphrases Isaiah 25:1–5 as a song of praise to God for protecting us. Check it out: "God, you are *my* God. I celebrate you. I praise you. You've done your share of miracle-wonders, well-thought-out plans, solid and sure. . . . Superpowers will see it and honor you, brutal oppressors bow in worshipful reverence. They'll see that you take care of the poor, that you take care of poor people in trouble, provide a warm, dry place in bad weather, provide a cool place when it's hot."

Can you write your own song of praise to Jesus

for protecting you? First, make a list of the ways that Jesus has protected you and your family in the past. Then make a poem out of your list, thanking God for all He's done. See if you can come up with a melody for your poem, and then you have your very own personal worship song to God. Ask Him for help as you write it out; His Holy Spirit is in you, making it all happen.

Lord, please give me the faith to believe in Your power to protect me. Thank You for protecting me and my family in the past. I trust that You'll do it again.

THINK ABOUT IT:

Who do you know who would be encouraged by your poem of praise? Think of ways to share your song of praise with others.

A REFUGE FROM THE STORM

You are a tower of refuge to the poor,
O Lord, a tower of refuge to the needy
in distress. You are a refuge from the
storm and a shelter from the heat.

Isaiah 25:4 NLT

Jesus is a refuge from the storm. A *refuge* is a place of safety and protection. The Bible tells us that Jesus Himself is our refuge.

Have you ever been outside when a storm came on suddenly? It can be a very scary experience! Wind and lightning can do great damage. The Bible tells us about a big storm that happened while Jesus and the disciples were on a boat. Jesus was asleep and the waves were sweeping up over the boat. The disciples thought they were going to drown! They went and woke up Jesus, begging for help. The good thing is that they went to the right person. Jesus spoke to the wind and waves and told them to stop. And they did! Isn't that amazing? Matthew 8:27 (NLV) tells us how the disciples responded: "They said, 'What kind of a man is He? Even the winds and the waves obey Him.'"

Jesus still holds the same power over all of nature today. He is a safe place from the storm. You can always ask Him for help. A family we know was traveling on the eastern plains of Colorado during a scary storm. They were on the flat highway and had nowhere to go. They pulled onto the side

44

of the road as large objects flew past them. They began to pray out loud for God's protection, and He heard them! Our friends were safe and unharmed. As cars began to ease back onto the road after the storm had passed, the family began to notice that most other cars passing them were missing their windows as the hail had broken through the glass. But our friends' car was intact with only hail damage on the outside and no broken glass!

When you're tempted to doubt God's power and love for you, remember that the winds and the waves still obey Him!

Jesus, You are my refuge and the safest place I can be. Thank You for hearing me when I pray.

THINK ABOUT IT:
Remember the last time you were scared about something. What does Jesus want you to know about that? Ask Him!

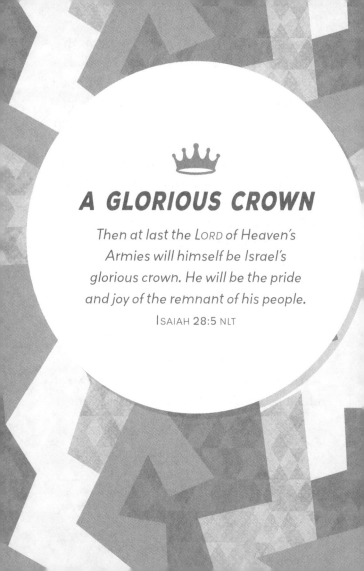

A GLORIOUS CROWN

Then at last the LORD of Heaven's Armies will himself be Israel's glorious crown. He will be the pride and joy of the remnant of his people.

ISAIAH 28:5 NLT

Have you ever dressed up as a king, queen, or princess? You could have the fanciest dress and best jewels, but if you don't have a crown...no one will know you're royalty, right? The crown tells people who you are.

The Bible tells us that Jesus Himself will be like our very own royal crown. BibleStudyTools.com tells us more about the meaning of "glorious crown" in this verse: "surrounding, adorning, and protecting his people; granting them his presence; giving them his grace, and large measures of it."

Since God is your Creator, only He can tell you who you really are. And being a child of the Most High God makes you royalty, crowned by Jesus Himself! Do you know how amazing that is?

There will come a time in your life when other people will make fun of you or put you down because of who they think you are—but you don't have to agree with any of that, nor let it bother you! Why? Because you are a prince or princess in God's kingdom. He says that you are loved and cherished and worth more than you could possibly imagine. Jesus wants you to take any lies or hurts that come at you and bring them to Him instead of agreeing with them and letting them have space in your head and in your heart. He will exchange those hurts and lies with the truth of who He says you are: His beloved child. Want to know what else He says about you? Take some time today to look up these scripture verses: Romans 8:31, 38–39; Galatians 5:1; Ephesians 2:18; 1 John 1:7.

Knowing who you are in Christ will change your whole life forever. Because of what Jesus has done for you, all of these things are true!

Jesus, You are my crown of glory!
I'm amazed at all You have done for me.
Thank You for showing me who I really am.

THINK ABOUT IT:
Which of the scriptures you looked
up meant the most to you and why?

OUR LAWGIVER

*For the L*ORD *is our judge, our lawgiver,
and our king. He will care for us and save us.*

ISAIAH **33:22** NLT

Have you ever been playing with a group of kids and one person decides to make up all the rules? A lot of times that can be really unfair. Kids can be mean and selfish, and sometimes they make up ridiculous rules that allow only the rule-maker to win.

The Bible tells us that Jesus is our Lawgiver. He is the only One who can see all sides and always plays fair or, in legal terms, just. Have you ever read parts of the Old Testament? It includes a ton of laws that seem like they would be impossible to keep. And people broke them all the time. God gave these laws to show the people how to live in a broken world and to show them their sin. Because God is holy and just, He does not tolerate sin. So the Israelite people had to make sacrifices before God so they could be acceptable to Him again. They would sacrifice, or give up, a lamb to be killed for their sins.

Jesus came to fulfill all of that. He became our sacrificial lamb, once and for all, making us right before God forever and ever. God sent Jesus to take the blame for all the sins of everyone.

His death on the cross for you accomplished that. Then He rose up from the grave and conquered death and sin for all time.

Jesus came to make you right with God so that when God looks at you, He sees the righteousness (the rightness, the perfectness) of Jesus. You are clean and free to live a great life, with Jesus guiding you and blessing you.

Wow, God! You see me as perfect because of Jesus? How awesome is that! Thank You for Your love and sacrifice for me. I love You, Lord Jesus!

THINK ABOUT IT:
How would it feel to have to make a sacrifice to God every time you sinned? What does Jesus want you to know about that now?

MY MAKER

*For your Maker is your husband,
the LORD of hosts is his name; and the
Holy One of Israel is your Redeemer,
the God of the whole earth he is called.*

ISAIAH 54:5 ESV

The book of John tells us so much about the life of Jesus. If you plan to read a whole book of the Bible, the book of John is a great one to start with. John was one of Jesus' twelve disciples, so he was there when all of this happened. We get the story from him firsthand. John begins by telling us that Jesus has been there from the beginning. This might be a little hard to understand, but Jesus has always existed, even before He was born! Wait—what?! Can anyone else say that?

Take a look at John 1:1–5 (NLV): "The Word (Christ) was in the beginning. The Word was with God. The Word was God. He was with God in the beginning. He made all things. Nothing was made without Him making it. Life began by Him. His Life was the Light for men. The Light shines in the darkness. The darkness has never been able to put out the Light."

Jesus was completely God and completely man. Jesus is the image of the invisible God (Colossians 1:15) who made the whole world. Jesus Christ made all things—and that means He made you too. So Jesus is your Maker. Did you know that?

And Colossians 2:9 (NLT) tells us, "For in Christ lives all the fullness of God in a human body."

The apostle Paul tells us a little more about this mystery in Ephesians 3:9 (NKJV): "the mystery, which from the beginning of the ages has been hidden in God who created all things through Jesus Christ."

When you put your trust in Jesus, you are putting your faith in the one true God—your Maker—who was and is and is to come (Revelation 1:8).

Jesus, I might not be able to comprehend everything about You, but I do put my faith and trust in You. I believe You are my Maker and the one true God.

THINK ABOUT IT:
Why do you think some things about God are still a great mystery to humans?

THE GOD OF THE WHOLE EARTH

For your Creator will be your husband;
the LORD of Heaven's Armies is his name!
He is your Redeemer, the Holy One of
Israel, the God of all the earth.

ISAIAH 54:5 NLT

The Bible tells us in the book of Genesis that God created the heavens and the earth. He is the Creator of all. As we learned in yesterday's reading, God created everything through Jesus Christ. So Jesus is the God of the whole earth. Let's answer some important questions about our world.

Did God create the universe and everything in it? Yep. He created the "heavens," meaning everything in our galaxy and more than one billion other galaxies that exist in our universe.

Why is earth and its people so special? Earth is where God decided to place humankind. God is love, and He created everything because of love. Creating earth and all the people on it was an expression of His great love.

Take a look at Genesis 1:26–27, 31 (NIV):

Then God said, "Let us make mankind in our image, in our likeness, so that they may rule over the fish in the sea and the birds in the sky, over the livestock and all the wild animals, and over all the creatures that move along the ground." So God created mankind in his own image, in the image of God he created them; male and female he created them.... God saw all that he had made, and it was very good.

Why did God make us? Because He wanted us to reach for Him and find His love, to be in relationship with Him. Acts 17:24–28 (NIV) explains it this way:

"The God who made the world and everything in it is the Lord of heaven and earth and does not live in temples built by human hands. And he is not served by human hands, as if he needed anything. Rather, he himself gives everyone life and breath and everything else. From one man he made all the nations, that they should inhabit the whole earth; and he marked out their appointed times in history and the boundaries of their lands. God did this so that they would seek him and perhaps reach out for him and find him, though he is not far from any one of us. 'For in him we live and move and have our being.'"

Thank You for creating me, reaching out for me, and loving me, Jesus!

THINK ABOUT IT:
What would it have been like to watch Jesus create the world?

A LEADER

*"See, I made him one who told of what
he had seen and heard to the nations,
a leader and ruler of the people."*

ISAIAH 55:4 NLV

Jesus was and is the greatest leader ever because He is a servant leader. See what Jesus Himself has to say about that: "Whoever wants to be a leader among you must be your servant, and whoever wants to be first among you must be the slave of everyone else. For even the Son of Man came not to be served but to serve others and to give his life as a ransom for many" (Mark 10:43–45 NLT).

In the book of John, we see Jesus washing the feet of His disciples before they ate (see John 13:1–17 if you want to know the whole story). Why in the world would Jesus do this? In Bible times, people would wear leather sandals and their feet would get very dirty, so usually a house servant would meet guests at the door and wash their feet before they entered. But Jesus showed that He was a humble servant leader by washing His disciples' feet Himself. They were astonished by His actions. Peter tried to get Him to stop! The most powerful man in history was stooping to do a servant's job. But Jesus did this on purpose. He wants His followers to be humble, loving, and willing to be misunderstood as they serve others out of love for God.

Loving leaders will put the needs of their followers before their own and serve others out of a thankful heart, knowing God will provide everything that is needed. We can give to others as God gives to us. Philippians 4:19 (NLT) says, "And this same God who takes care of me will supply all your needs from his glorious riches, which have been given to us in Christ Jesus."

When we take time to seek Jesus first and trust Him to care for all our needs, He gives us the strength, courage, and supplies to serve others in love.

Jesus, You are the very best leader. Please fill me with Your Spirit so I can lead like You do.

THINK ABOUT IT: How does it make you feel when someone serves you out of love? Can you be a leader like that too?

THE EVERLASTING LIGHT

Your sun will never set; your moon will not go down. For the Lord will be your everlasting light. Your days of mourning will come to an end.

Isaiah 60:20 NLT

The Lord Jesus is our everlasting light. John 1:9–12 (NIV) says:

"The true light that gives light to everyone was coming into the world. He was in the world, and though the world was made through him, the world did not recognize him. He came to that which was his own, but his own did not receive him. Yet to all who did receive him, to those who believed in his name, he gave the right to become children of God."

This verse means that Jesus is the light and He brought His light to all people. If you accept Jesus and allow His light to glow in you, you become a child of God.

John 8:12 (NIV) says, "When Jesus spoke again to the people, he said, 'I am the light of the world. Whoever follows me will never walk in darkness, but will have the light of life.'" An amazing thing happens when you choose to follow Jesus: His Spirit comes to live inside of you to light up your life.

Do you have any candles decorating your house? They might be nice to look at on their own, but when you light them with a match or a lighter, the fire makes them become powerful, producing light and heat. That's kind of how it is with God's Spirit in us. You probably have natural ability to do a lot of things on your own, but with God's power you can do so much more! Second Corinthians 4:7 (NLV) tells us, "We have this light from God in our human bodies. This shows that the power is from God. It is not from ourselves."

God wants to help you live in His everlasting light. Ask Him to help you shine your light in dark places.

Jesus, thank You for filling my heart with Your everlasting light. Help me to carry Your light with me wherever I go.

THINK ABOUT IT:
Is the everlasting light of Jesus shining in you? How do you know?

OUR POTTER

And yet, O Lᴏʀᴅ, you are our Father.
We are the clay, and you are the potter.
We all are formed by your hand.

Isaiah 64:8 NLT

Have you ever taken a lump of clay and tried to make something nice out of it? If you've ever seen a master potter at work, you probably thought they made it look easy! But once you've tried it yourself, you know how incredibly difficult it is to work lumpy clay into something nice. It takes lots and lots of practice to get it right. Ask your parents to show you a video of a potter making a fine piece of pottery. It's amazing how they take a tough, unformed lump of clay and transform it into something lovely. That's what God wants to do with us, if we'll let Him!

The potter adds water to the hard clay and works it into the lump until it becomes pliable. Then he begins the slow process of shaping the clay into what he wants it to become. The lump doesn't get to decide—the potter does.

Jesus is the Master Potter. When we say yes to Him, His Spirit comes alive inside of us, transforming our hearts and minds into something useful and lovely! Second Corinthians 4:7 (NIV) says, "We have this treasure in jars of clay to show that this all-surpassing power is from God and not from us."

Jesus has great plans for your life. He has given you unique talents and abilities that tell of His glory inside you. Come to Jesus, the Master Potter, and allow Him to shape you into everything He has designed for you to be.

Jesus, I trust You with my life.
Please soften my heart and mold
me to be what You have designed.

THINK ABOUT IT:

If you were a potter, what would
you make with a lump of clay?

MY PHYSICIAN

Is there no medicine in Gilead? Is there no physician there? Why is there no healing for the wounds of my people?

JEREMIAH 8:22 NLT

esus is the Great Physician. Mark 6:56 (NLV) says, "Wherever He went, they would lay the sick people in the streets in the center of town where people gather. They begged Him that they might touch the bottom of His coat. Everyone who did was healed."

Wherever Jesus went, crowds of people would follow. They knew Jesus had the power to heal. The crowds would lay sick people in the streets for Jesus to touch. Imagine people who had been sick their whole lives, desperate to be free of their illness. Imagine people who couldn't see or hear and people who couldn't walk. They heard that Jesus had power. They didn't understand it yet, but they wanted to be well. And they would do just about anything even just to touch the coat of Jesus. Jesus knew the state of their hearts and He had loving compassion for them. He could've healed everyone on earth instantly, but He waited for the people to come to Him.

A woman who'd had a bleeding disorder for twelve years came to Jesus secretly. She was labeled as "unclean" by her society. She reached out for Jesus and touched His clothes. She was healed instantly. She tried to slip away unnoticed, but Jesus called to her. Take a look: "Then Jesus turned around. He saw her and said, 'Daughter, take hope! Your faith has healed you.' At once the woman was healed" (Matthew 9:22 NLV).

Maybe Jesus wanted her to know that His clothes didn't have miraculous powers but it was her faith in God that healed her. Maybe He wanted the crowd to know that just because a person has been labeled, they are still worthy of love and respect. Either way, this woman showed simple faith in a miraculous God, and she was healed.

Jesus, Thank You for Your healing power.
I trust that You are a God of miracles and
that my simple faith in You is enough.

THINK ABOUT IT:
Do you think it's more important for God to heal our hearts or our bodies?

RESTING PLACE

"My people have become lost sheep. Their shepherds have led them the wrong way. They have made them turn away on the mountains. They have gone from mountain to hill and have forgotten their resting place."

Jeremiah 50:6 nlv

*J*esus is our resting place. What an amazing name of Jesus to hold on to. Matthew 11:28–30 (NIV) says, "Come to me, all you who are weary and burdened, and I will give you rest. Take my yoke upon you and learn from me, for I am gentle and humble in heart, and you will find rest for your souls. For my yoke is easy and my burden is light."

Jesus wants you to come to Him about every. . .single. . .thing. He wants to share your whole life with you. The good, the bad, the easy and fun, the difficult and heavy. He offers to give your soul a rest. A deep soul rest is the kind you need when you're really tired from trying to make everyone happy. Does your soul need a rest? Have you had a hard time trying to please others, like your parents, your teachers, your friends? Sometimes being a kid is hard and you can get worn out. It may seem like people are always trying to tell you what to do. And you can be pretty hard on yourself too, right? Maybe you like things to be perfect and sometimes they just aren't!

Jesus wants you to know that you can find the

perfect rest in Him. You don't have to work hard to please Him. He just wants to be your friend. He wants you to find all of your answers in Him and through Him. . .by going to Him first. When you start doing that, you'll see that He gives you rest, peace, love, answers, strength, courage— absolutely everything you might need!

The Message paraphrases Matthew 11:28–30 this way: "Come to me. Get away with me and you'll recover your life. . . . I won't lay anything heavy or ill-fitting on you. Keep company with me and you'll learn to live freely and lightly."

Living freely and lightly sounds pretty good, right? So come to Him. Bring Him all your thoughts and feelings. He cares so much for you!

Jesus, help me to come to You first.
Be my resting place.

THINK ABOUT IT:
How can you remember to go to Jesus first about everything that matters to you?

THE HOPE OF HIS PEOPLE

The LORD also shall roar out of Zion, and utter his voice from Jerusalem; and the heavens and the earth shall shake: but the LORD will be the hope of his people, and the strength of the children of Israel.

JOEL 3:16 KJV

Life isn't easy. Not even when you're a kid. Growing up is hard work. Jesus knows this! He had to grow up too! He wants you to know that He understands everything you are going through. Jesus is the Hope of His People. And that means He is your hope too! He is there for you, waiting to help you through every situation. Jesus gives us a ton of hope and encouragement in His Word. Check these out:

> ► "May the God of hope fill you with all joy and peace as you trust in him, so that you may overflow with hope by the power of the Holy Spirit" (Romans 15:13 NIV).

> ► "I have told you these things so you may have peace in Me. In the world you will have much trouble. But take hope! I have power over the world!" (John 16:33 NLV).

> ► "Have I not commanded you? Be strong and courageous. Do not be afraid; do not be discouraged, for the LORD your God will be with you wherever you go" (Joshua 1:9 NIV).

> ► "It's a good thing to quietly hope, quietly hope for help from GOD. It's a good

thing when you're young to stick it out through the hard times"
(Lamentations 3:26–27 MSG).

▶ "For I am the LORD your God who takes hold of your right hand and says to you, Do not fear; I will help you" (Isaiah 41:13 NIV).

▶ "No, in all these things we are more than conquerors through him who loved us" (Romans 8:37 NIV).

▶ "Since God assured us, 'I'll never let you down, never walk off and leave you,' we can boldly quote, 'God is there, ready to help; I'm fearless no matter what. Who or what can get to me?'" (Hebrews 13:5–6 MSG).

Jesus, I'm so glad You understand my life! Thanks for helping me. Please fill me with joy and hope that overflows.

THINK ABOUT IT:
Which verse speaks into your life the most? Why?

THE KING

Then everyone who is left of all the nations that went against Jerusalem will go each year to worship the King, the Lord of All, and to keep the Special Supper of Tents.

ZECHARIAH 14:16 NLV

Jesus is the King of all kings. He was born in a lowly stable, He grew up and died a criminal's death on a cross because of His great love for us, and then He conquered death and rose to life and is now seated at the right hand of God in heaven.

He has power over all things and if you have become His child by choosing to love and follow Him, He will never let you go or let you down. Romans 8:28 (NLV) says, "We know that God makes all things work together for the good of those who love Him and are chosen to be a part of His plan."

Sometimes we need a good reminder of what God is doing in our lives. So here it is: God is with you always. He is listening and He loves you like you're the only kid in the universe! You are His kid and He will never abandon you. He has set His own Spirit alive inside your heart. You are a child of the King of all kings, and He has wonderful plans for your life. Even the painful things that happen in life, God can miraculously turn into good things if you trust in Him!

As you grow up, you're going to face a lot of distractions in life, trying to get you to turn away from trusting in God's great love for you and in your royal status in His kingdom. That's our enemy's purpose in this life. So remember how much God loves you and hide Romans 8:28 in your heart. Memorize it and allow the Holy Spirit to bring it to your mind anytime you start to forget. The great King is working out everything for your good and for His glory.

Jesus, thank You for being the King of my heart. I'm so amazed and thankful that You call me Your child—a prince or princess in Your kingdom. Help me take that status seriously and serve You well.

THINK ABOUT IT:
What does your "royal status" mean to you? Do you believe you are royalty?

JESUS

"A Son will be born to her. You will give Him the name Jesus because He will save His people from the punishment of their sins."

Matthew 1:21 nlv

Pastor and author Max Lucado wrote a book called *God Came Near*.* He tells us how the name "Jesus" was a common name during the time that Jesus walked the earth. It might be the same as "Joe" is today. As we now know, Jesus was and is the King of all kings! And yet He wanted to come and be involved in the lives of everyday people. He could've come to earth and demanded a golden palace. He owns everything, after all. He could've demanded that everyone bow to Him in service and submission. But He wanted to be friends instead. He wanted regular people to feel comfortable around Him.

People loved to be around Jesus. They even wanted their children to be near Him! Why? Because He didn't make Himself seem more important than them. He was just Jesus—and how could anyone be afraid of someone who loved and welcomed everyone?

Jesus wants you to know that you can always come to Him, still. And you will never be turned away. In John 15:13–15 (MSG), Jesus says,

"This is my command: Love one another the way I loved you. This is the very best way to love.

Put your life on the line for your friends. You are my friends when you do the things I command you. I'm no longer calling you servants because servants don't understand what their master is thinking and planning. No, I've named you friends because I've let you in on everything I've heard from the Father."

Jesus, I'm so thankful that I can come to You with anything and I will never be rejected. You are the best friend I could ever have. Thank You for Your love.

THINK ABOUT IT:

Can you imagine Jesus as a young boy? What would it have been like to be His friend?

*Max Lucado, God Came Near (Nashville, TN: Thomas Nelson, 2004).

IMMANUEL

He said, "The young woman, who has never had a man, will give birth to a Son. They will give Him the name Immanuel. This means God with us."

<small>Matthew 1:23 nlv</small>

Jesus is Immanuel. You've probably heard this name before, especially at Christmastime in the songs of the season. This special name was foretold way back in the Old Testament in the book of Isaiah, hundreds and hundreds of years before Jesus was born (see Isaiah 7:14). God had a rescue plan in place for His people.

God's people made a lot of mistakes. Big ones. They allowed selfishness and sin to take over ever since that infamous day when Eve took a bite of the apple in the Garden of Eden and shared some with Adam. None of this was a surprise to God, of course. He knows all and He gave humans the ability to choose.

You wouldn't want to create something that was forced to love you, right? That would be like having a robot. You can't have a real relationship with a robot. Having the ability to choose is called "free will"—and free will is messy. Relationships are messy. Love is messy. God knows this. And He chose to create us and love us anyway. That's who He is. A Creator. The very source of love.

The benefits and beauty of true love far outweigh the heartache and pain. There's an old saying that it's better to love and get hurt than never to know love at all.

And God sent His own Son to be the rescue for humankind's sin.

John 3:16–17 (NIV) tells us why: "For God so loved the world that he gave his one and only Son, that whoever believes in him shall not perish but have eternal life. For God did not send his Son into the world to condemn the world, but to save the world through him."

God became one of us. Immanuel.

Jesus, I'm amazed that You became one of us. Thank You for knowing me fully and loving me anyway.

THINK ABOUT IT:

Have you ever been hurt by someone you love? Do you think it would've been better never to have loved that person in the first place?

FRIEND OF SINNERS

"The Son of Man came eating and drinking, and they say, 'Here is a glutton and a drunkard, a friend of tax collectors and sinners.' But wisdom is proved right by her deeds."

MATTHEW 11:19 NIV

As we've been learning, Jesus was an everyday guy. He was a hardworking man and He made friends with regular people. One day, He went to visit a man named Matthew, a tax collector. Matthew was hated by the Jewish people because tax collectors back then were known for cheating people. Jesus had dinner with Matthew and some of the tax collector's friends. The Pharisees asked the disciples why their teacher would do such a terrible thing as eat with tax collectors and sinners. Jesus heard them and said, "People who are well do not need a doctor. But go and understand these words, 'I want loving-kindness and not a gift to be given.' For I have not come to call good people. I have come to call those who are sinners" (Matthew 9:12–13 NLV).

Jesus wisely responded that it's sick people who need a doctor, not healthy people. Jesus was a friend of sinners and a doctor to the sick. That means that He had the healing and the answers that sinful people needed to change their lives. Jesus asked Matthew to follow Him, so he left his sinful job and did what Jesus asked. Jesus had the answers Matthew needed. He has the answers for our sinful world too.

Pray for the people around you who need Jesus, and ask for opportunities to share God's love with them. Do you think this means that Jesus wants you to be friends with people who make really bad choices and do what they do? Be loving and kind, yes. Do what they do? Nope. As followers of Jesus, we are called to be a light in the darkness. To make better choices because of the love in our hearts for God.

Jesus, please fill me with loving-kindness for the people around me. Even the ones who are hard to love. Help me be a friend and a good example to all those who need You.

THINK ABOUT IT:

Are there people in your life who are hard to love? How can you show them the love of Jesus?

MASTER

"A faithful, sensible servant is one to whom the master can give the responsibility of managing his other household servants and feeding them. If the master returns and finds that the servant has done a good job, there will be a reward."

MATTHEW 24:45–46 NLT

*T*he word *master* can have several meanings. In Bible times, there were plenty of servants and masters. Today, thankfully, slavery is outlawed in most of the world. *Master* is another name for someone who is really good at something, like a master violinist or a master artist.

Jesus is our Master, and we serve Him out of love. Jesus told a story about a master and his good and faithful servant. This story is called the parable of the talents. Back in Bible times, a talent was a large sum of money. A landowner was going on a big trip, so he divided up his money and gave it to his servants according to their abilities. One servant was given five talents, another servant was given two talents, and the last one was given one talent. The man who was given five talents went right to work with that money and earned five more. "His owner said to him, 'You have done well. You are a good and faithful servant. You have been faithful over a few things. I will put many things in your care. Come and share my joy' " (Matthew 25:21 NLV).

The one who was given two talents earned two

more. The master was happy with this servant too. But the last servant was afraid that something bad would happen to his talent, so he buried it and didn't earn a thing. He did nothing for his master and got in trouble for it.

Jesus is a good Master. He understands our hearts and our decisions. He also wants us to share in His joy. Jesus has given each of us certain gifts and talents, and He wants us to use them to honor God and bless others. How are you using the gifts God has given you?

Jesus, I'm happy to call you my Master. You are the only One worthy to be called such a name. Thanks for loving me so well.

THINK ABOUT IT:
The parable of the talents has a double meaning. Can you think about what this means for your life?

THE CARPENTER

"Is He not a Man Who makes things from wood? Is He not the Son of Mary and the brother of James and Joses and Judas and Simon? Do not His sisters live here with us?" The people were ashamed of Him and turned away from Him.

MARK 6:3 NLV

Biblical scholars are people who study the Bible as their job. They've had a lot of discussion about this verse over the years. Some say Jesus was a carpenter, meaning He made things out of wood. Others say that there were, and are, a lot more rocks in Jesus' hometown than trees, so he was more likely a stonemason who crafted things out of stone. Either way, they can agree on the main idea: Jesus was a master builder. He crafted things out of wood or stone, shaping them into something useful. And He is still doing that today.

Are you a creative kid? Do you like to take a bunch of materials and craft them into something beautiful or useful? Or maybe you like building things with Legos. It's fun to have an idea in your imagination and watch it come to life through your very own hands.

Jesus was a builder. He was a regular guy with a regular job, but He was also God in a human body. The man who could've snapped His fingers and made a chair or a house in an instant, patiently worked with the materials He had and shaped them into what He wanted them to become.

Jesus wants to shape us into all He wants us to be too. Jeremiah 29:11–13 (NLT) says, "'For I know the plans I have for you,' says the LORD. 'They are plans for good and not for disaster, to give you a future and a hope. In those days when you pray, I will listen. If you look for me wholeheartedly, you will find me.'"

Jesus has a good plan for your life. He wants you to seek Him and find Him. And as you learn to go to Him for everything, He'll continue to shape you and lead you into His amazing plans for your life.

Jesus, teach me how to come to You for everything. I want Your good plans for my life.

THINK ABOUT IT:

Why do you think the Father wanted Jesus to have a regular job while He was on earth?

THE SON OF MARY

*"Is this not the carpenter, the Son of Mary,
and brother of James, Joses, Judas,
and Simon? And are not His sisters here
with us?" So they were offended at Him.*

MARK 6:3 NKJV

J esus was the Son of Mary. The Bible tells us that the Holy Spirit came upon Mary and caused her to be pregnant with Jesus. Jesus had no real earthly father because Joseph was His stepdad. Jesus grew up in a small farming community called Nazareth. It was most likely looked down upon by other, wealthier cities and towns.

After Jesus grew up and it was time to begin His ministry, He went away from His hometown to be baptized by John. Mark 1:10–11 (NLT) says, "As Jesus came up out of the water, he saw the heavens splitting apart and the Holy Spirit descending on him like a dove. And a voice from heaven said, 'You are my dearly loved Son, and you bring me great joy.' "

Can you imagine being part of that crowd watching Jesus get baptized and suddenly, out of the sky, you hear a voice? How amazing and scary! Yes, Jesus was the Son of Mary, but as Jesus was getting baptized, God the Father told everyone watching who Jesus really is—the Son of God.

Jesus called His disciples to join Him and went around to other towns and villages healing people and telling them that the kingdom of God had come near. Some time later, He finally headed back to His hometown where everybody knew Him. He started teaching in church, but the people had a hard time believing anything He said. They knew His mom. They knew His whole family. How could a regular guy like Jesus do miracles? "Jesus told them, 'A prophet has little honor in his hometown, among his relatives, on the streets he played in as a child.' Jesus wasn't able to do much of anything there—he laid hands on a few sick people and healed them, that's all. He couldn't get over their stubbornness" (Mark 6:4–6 MSG).

The people of Jesus' hometown had very little faith, and so He chose to move on to people who would accept Him.

Jesus, please make my faith in You grow.

THINK ABOUT IT:
Why is your faith in Jesus so important?

GOD MY SAVIOR

*"And my spirit has rejoiced
in God my Savior."*

LUKE 1:47 NKJV

Jesus didn't come to condemn us; He came to save us. He is our Savior. He died on the cross to take away all the sins of the world. Remember John 3:16–17. Do you have that passage memorized yet? The ancient philosopher Augustine said that "God loves each of us as if there were only one of us." And when we believe and receive Christ as our Lord and Savior, we are guaranteed a life that lasts forever. Making Jesus Lord of our life means that we choose to let Him lead us throughout our life. We follow His Word and His ways.

John 1:12 (NLV) says, "He gave the right and the power to become children of God to those who received Him. He gave this to those who put their trust in His name."

When you receive Jesus as your Savior, you become a child of God. Verse 13 (NLV) says that you become "born of God." Can you believe it? When you are born as a baby, you come alive physically. When you are "born of God," you come alive spiritually. The day you accepted Jesus as your Savior is your spiritual birthday. It's something fun and important to celebrate! If you know when you asked Jesus into your heart, write down the day and plan a celebration. If you don't know the exact day, ask your family to help you estimate so you have a close idea.

Becoming a child of God comes with a huge inheritance! First Peter 1:4 (NLT) tells us, "We have a priceless inheritance—an inheritance that is kept in heaven for you, pure and undefiled, beyond the reach of change and decay." We don't know what all this includes, but we do know that Jesus is the High King and we are His children. Our inheritance will be beyond our imagination.

Jesus, You've offered me a life that lasts forever, and I accept. You are my Savior, and I am so blessed that You chose me to be Your child.

THINK ABOUT IT:
What do you think your inheritance
in heaven will look like?

HORN OF SALVATION

"And has raised up a horn of salvation for us in the house of His servant David."

LUKE 1:69 NKJV

Jesus is our horn of salvation! What could that possibly mean? Let's take a look at two psalms that can help us understand:

> ▶ "The LORD is my rock, my fortress, and the One who rescues me; my God, my rock and strength in whom I trust and take refuge; my shield, and the horn of my salvation, my high tower—my stronghold" (Psalm 18:2 AMP).

> ▶ "There I will make the horn (strength) of David grow; I have prepared a lamp for My anointed [fulfilling the promises]" (Psalm 132:17 AMP).

After reading those verses, what do you think the Bible is telling us about Jesus being the horn of salvation?

Did you guess strength? If so, you're right! Jesus is our strength.

A woman named Corrie ten Boom was put in prison during World War II for helping Jews escape the Nazis by hiding them in a closet in her home. She was a watchmaker and an author who learned to put her trust in Jesus. She said, "Trying to do the Lord's work in your own strength is the most confusing, exhausting, and tedious of all work. But when you are filled with the Holy Spirit, then the ministry of Jesus just flows out of you."

Jesus promised to send us the Holy Spirit. . . and He did. But we have to accept the help of God's Spirit. He wants us to be filled with His Spirit to remind us of everything Jesus said. The Holy Spirit will remind us how loved we are. He will help us hear from God. He will give us wisdom and strength. If you are feeling tired and like you can't keep going, remember this: "The Lord will always lead you. He will satisfy your needs in dry lands. He will give strength to your bones. You will be like a garden that has much water. You will be like a spring that never runs dry" (Isaiah 58:11 ICB).

Jesus, I need Your strength in my life.
Remind me to come to You when I feel tired.

THINK ABOUT IT:
Are you feeling tired or worn out
about something? What is it?

CHRIST THE LORD

"Today, One Who saves from the punishment of sin has been born in the city of David. He is Christ the Lord."

LUKE 2:11 NLV

Jesus is Christ the Lord. Let's look at a bunch of things that God wants us to know about Jesus that you might not have known before. Take a look:

- ▶ Jesus is the Son of God (Mark 1:1).

- ▶ Jesus came so that we could know God (John 1:18).

- ▶ Jesus came to save us from our sins so we can live forever (John 3:16–17).

- ▶ Jesus is the image of the invisible God (Colossians 1:15).

- ▶ Jesus is the only way to God (John 14:6).

- ▶ Jesus loves you (John 15:9)!

Now, some of these facts about Jesus might be confusing. But that's because God is *so big*, we can't possibly understand everything about Him. But here's the amazing thing: whenever you have a question about Jesus, you can just ask Him! Matthew 11:25 (NIV) tells us, "At that time Jesus said, 'I praise you, Father, Lord of heaven and earth, because you have hidden these things from the wise and learned, and revealed them to little children.'"

You are so special to Jesus. He wants to tell

you important things about Himself that take the faith of a child to understand. Here are a few other things God wants you to know about our Lord Jesus:

▶ "The Lord came to us from far away, saying, 'I have loved you with a love that lasts forever. So I have helped you come to Me with loving-kindness'" (Jeremiah 31:3 NLV).

▶ "All your children will be taught by the LORD, and great will be their peace" (Isaiah 54:13 NIV).

▶ "The much-loved Son is beside the Father. 'No man has ever seen God. But Christ has made God known to us'" (John 1:18 NLV).

Jesus, be the Lord of my life. I'm so thankful You want me to know who You are. Please work in my heart as I learn more about You. Help me to trust You.

THINK ABOUT IT:
What does it mean for Jesus
to be the Lord of your life?

THE BABE

"And this will be the sign to you: You will find a Babe wrapped in swaddling cloths, lying in a manger."

LUKE 2:12 NKJV

This message of Jesus, the Babe, was given to a group of shepherds. You've probably heard this story at Christmas, right?

> And there were shepherds living out in the fields nearby, keeping watch over their flocks at night. An angel of the Lord appeared to them, and the glory of the Lord shone around them, and they were terrified. But the angel said to them, "Do not be afraid. I bring you good news that will cause great joy for all the people. Today in the town of David a Savior has been born to you; he is the Messiah, the Lord. This will be a sign to you: You will find a baby wrapped in cloths and lying in a manger." (Luke 2:8–12 NIV)

The Jews had been waiting for a Savior for ages and ages. They wanted to be saved from the Roman rulers who bullied them. But God had something much more important in store for the whole world. This baby would grow up, live, and die to save all of humanity from their sins. God Himself had come to earth as a human baby.

Author Dorothy Sayers wrote this: "He was not merely a man so good as to be 'like God'—He was God. . . ." *Jesus knew what it was like to live in a family; He knew what hard work was like; He suffered pain; He experienced humiliation and death. And He did all of it for You—and for every human being ever born!

The baby Jesus grew up and gave His life for us. He has experienced every human emotion that we have (Hebrews 4:15). He did all of this because of love. He came to be one of us.

Jesus, I'm sad for all that You went through because of me. But I'm so thankful too. You gave Your life because of Your great love for me.

THINK ABOUT IT:
Why do you think Jesus thought it was worthwhile to be born as a human being?

*Dorothy Sayers, "The Greatest Drama Ever Staged" (London: Hodder & Stoughton, 1938).

A SIGN

Then Simeon blessed them, and he said to Mary, the baby's mother, "This child is destined to cause many in Israel to fall, and many others to rise. He has been sent as a sign from God, but many will oppose him."

LUKE 2:34 NLT

When Jesus was just over one week old, Mary and Joseph took Him to the temple to be consecrated to God. This was the Jewish custom. There were two older prophets at the temple who gave a prophecy over Jesus. A prophecy is a divine or God-given prediction of the future. A prophet was someone who spoke the truth of God. Simeon was an old man when he told Mary that Jesus was a sign from God. Simeon knew that this baby was the Messiah, the Savior of the world. Anna, an elderly woman prophetess, also knew that this baby was the promised Savior. She was one of the first people to start sharing the Good News that the Messiah had come.

We don't know much about how Jesus grew up except what it says right here: "And the child grew and became strong; he was filled with wisdom, and the grace of God was on him" (Luke 2:40 NIV).

We also know that when Jesus was twelve years old, He went to the temple and listened to the teachers, amazing them with His understanding (2:47). And then finally we read: "And Jesus grew in wisdom and stature, and in favor with God and man" (2:52 NIV).

That's all we hear about the boyhood of Jesus. For the next eighteen years, we only know that Jesus grew up, was educated, and loved His family and friends. The Savior of the whole world needed to grow up, go to school, learn a trade, and love others well.

What do you think that means for you? Does Jesus want you to follow a similar path? Growing in wisdom and favor was important before Jesus could start His ministry. Can you imagine Jesus learning how to do math? He has been through all the things that you have to go through as you grow up too.

Jesus, I'm glad You understand all the things I'm going through. Thanks for being close to me.

THINK ABOUT IT:

Why do you think the grown-ups in the temple were amazed at twelve-year-old Jesus?

THE WORD

*In the beginning the Word already
existed. The Word was with God,
and the Word was God.*

JOHN 1:1 NLT

Here's something to keep in mind as you grow in your faith. When you have trouble understanding a certain scripture verse, it helps to read it in a few different Bible translations to get a better picture of what God is saying. Take a look at these verses in the Amplified Bible and see if it helps you understand this interesting fact about Jesus being called "the Word": "In the beginning [before all time] was the Word (Christ), and the Word was with God, and the Word was God Himself. He was [continually existing] in the beginning [co-eternally] with God. All things were made and came into existence through Him; and without Him not even one thing was made that has come into being" (John 1:1–3 AMP).

Now take a look at verse 14 in the New International Version: "The Word became flesh and made his dwelling among us. We have seen his glory, the glory of the one and only Son, who came from the Father, full of grace and truth."

In Bible times, "the Word" meant quite a few different things: it was an expression used for God, His message to the world, and the Creator of all things. God was telling the world that Jesus Christ is all of those things. *He* is the very Word of God, God Himself, and God's message to the world sent in a human body.

This is some *big* stuff for a kid to understand! You're becoming a theologian (ask your parents what that big word means)! When big things like this come up while you're reading the Bible, pause for just a minute and close your eyes. Ask Jesus what He wants you to know about these things. Ready? Give it a try right now. . . .

When you pause and ask Jesus for answers, you'll find that He loves to answer you in *so* many amazing and creative ways! Sometimes He'll pop a picture right into your mind! Sometimes you'll remember a scripture verse. Other times a worship song will come to mind. Just keep paying attention!

Jesus, what do You want me to know about You being the Word? Please show me.

THINK ABOUT IT:
What are some other ways
God can speak to you?

THE LAMB OF GOD

The next day John saw Jesus coming toward him and said, "Look, the Lamb of God, who takes away the sin of the world!"

JOHN 1:29 NIV

Remember when we talked about Jesus being our Lawgiver on pages 49–51? We learned that Jesus became our sacrificial lamb once and for all, making us right before God forever and ever. We never have to make a sacrifice for our sins. Jesus did it. Once for all time. He became the Lamb of God who takes away the sins of the whole world.

Does that mean that everybody automatically gets into heaven? Nope. God gave us all free will. We each have to choose if we will trust in Jesus and accept the fact that He paid for our sins. Just because your mom or dad or grandma or grandpa believes in Jesus or goes to church doesn't mean that you get to go to heaven. We each have to make our own choices about Jesus.

Will you accept Jesus as the Lamb of God? Do you believe that He died to forgive all of your sins? If so, take a minute to thank Him again for all that He has done for you! If you've already asked Jesus into your heart, celebrate that you get to live forever and ever with Jesus and all of the people who love Him!

If you've never asked Jesus to forgive you for your sins and chosen to follow Him, are you ready now? If yes, it's so simple! Confess your sins to Jesus—that just means to agree with God that you've made mistakes and believe that He died to take those away forever. Then accept Him by inviting Him into your heart to be your friend and guide forever. Making Jesus the King of your heart is the best decision you will ever make.

It's been said that there is a God-shaped hole in every human heart—and nothing can fill it but our Creator God.

*Jesus, thank You for coming into
my heart. I choose to follow You!*

THINK ABOUT IT:
Do you think everyone has a God-shaped vacuum (hole) in their heart? Why or why not?

THE BREAD OF LIFE

Jesus replied, "I am the bread of life. Whoever comes to me will never be hungry again. Whoever believes in me will never be thirsty."

JOHN 6:35 NLT

Have you ever made homemade bread before? It smells so yummy as it's baking and fresh from the oven. Back in Bible times, each family had to make their own bread. It could take two or three hours just to make enough bread for each family for one day. Bread was often their main food and they needed it every day.

Jesus says He is our Bread of Life. Just as the people of the Bible had to make fresh bread every day, Jesus wants us to come to Him every day by talking to Him and reading His Word. We eat every day to keep our bodies healthy and growing. We eat spiritual food from Jesus so our faith can grow!

Ask your parents if they will help you gather the ingredients to make your own homemade bread. As you're preparing and baking, ask Jesus to fill your heart with His truth and love.

Does your church celebrate communion? They might call it something different like the Lord's Supper. Jesus asked us to remember Him in this way. "Then Jesus took bread and gave thanks and broke it in pieces. He gave it to them, saying,

'This is My body which is given for you. Do this to remember Me' " (Luke 22:19 NLV).

We have bread to remember the body of Jesus. He calls Himself the "bread of life." We have wine or juice to remember the blood of Jesus that was shed for us on the cross. He gave up His life to save us.

Plan a communion service at home with your family. Use the bread that you made. Read a few scriptures and sing some worship songs too!

Jesus, we remember You as a family. Thank You for Your sacrifice for us. Thank You for meeting our daily needs for physical food and spiritual food. We love You, Jesus.

THINK ABOUT IT:

Jesus wants our hearts to be right with Him before we take communion. Look up 1 Corinthians 11:27–30 and talk about what this means as a family.

I AM

"Believe me," said Jesus, "I am who I am long before Abraham was anything."

JOHN 8:58 MSG

Jesus told the Jewish leaders that He was "I am." That seems like only half of a sentence, right? What did it mean? Let's take a look. Exodus 3:14–15 (NIV) says, "God said to Moses, 'I AM WHO I AM. This is what you are to say to the Israelites: "I AM has sent me to you."'... This is my name for-ever, the name you shall call me from generation to generation.'"

The Jewish people knew that this name, I AM, was a holy name for God. So when Jesus called Himself "I AM," He caused quite a stir. In fact, the Jewish leaders accused Him of blasphemy, a crime against God. Jesus clearly told everyone that He was alive before Abraham. They had a hard time believing this, because Jesus was only around thirty years old!

Living a life of faith means that we often have to look beyond what we can see with our eyes and trust that God is real and alive in our hearts. Think about a really windy day. Wind can cause all kinds of things to happen, right? But can you see it with your eyes? Nope. You can see the effects of the wind and how it blows the trees, but wind itself is invisible (unless it's dusty out). Faith is the same way.

The Jewish leaders and Pharisees of Jesus' day could not see with eyes of faith. They saw only the facts. But sometimes even facts aren't exactly what they seem. Yep, Jesus was the son of Mary. Yep, He grew up in a poor town and had brothers and sisters. His physical age at that time was around thirty-two or thirty-three years old. But the whole truth is a lot different, right? Jesus was actually the Son of God who has been alive forever!

Jesus, please open my spiritual eyes so that I can see with eyes of faith. I know You're the God of miracles.

THINK ABOUT IT:

Can you think of a time when the facts weren't exactly what they seemed? What happened?

THE WAY

*Jesus answered, "I am the way and
the truth and the life. No one comes
to the Father except through me."*

JOHN 14:6 NIV

As you grow up, you may hear the words "All roads lead to heaven." But Jesus tells us that is not true. Take a look: "Go in through the narrow door. The door is wide and the road is easy that leads to hell. Many people are going through that door. But the door is narrow and the road is hard that leads to life that lasts forever. Few people are finding it" (Matthew 7:13–14 NLV).

That can be a hard passage to read. Heaven and hell are real places. Jesus tells us clearly that there is a narrow door to eternal life and that door is Jesus Himself. Jesus is the Way. It's one of His names. And He is the only way to heaven.

There are a lot of people in this world who live to satisfy their selfish desires. And the Bible tells us we reap what we sow. Let me explain: You probably know that whatever kind of seed you put in the ground is the kind of plant that will grow. How silly it would be if you planted peas but pumpkins grew instead! In the Bible, this is called sowing and reaping. You get back whatever you plant. This is true in the garden of our hearts too. If you plant selfishness. . .what is going to grow? What do you need to plant in your heart if you want to reap blessings instead? There are rewards for sowing good things and consequences for sowing evil.

There are also a lot of good people in this world who simply don't know that Jesus is the Way. So our job is to love Jesus, love others, and be exactly who He created us to be. When people see that we have a real, everyday friendship with Jesus, they are going to want to know the Way for themselves.

Jesus, help me to be the person who shines a bright light toward the narrow door! I want to show Your love to others so they can get to know the real You.

THINK ABOUT IT:
What do sowing and reaping have to do with eternal life?

THE TRUTH

Jesus answered, "I am the way and the truth and the life. No one comes to the Father except through me."

John 14:6 NIV

Jesus had a lot of followers who believed He was the Son of God. But He also had a lot of opponents who mocked Him, betrayed Him, and cursed Him. They simply could not believe that He was the Son of God, come to save the world from their sins. But Jesus always tells the truth. In fact, one of His names *is* Truth.

Take a look at this true story of what happened when Jesus died on the cross: "At once the curtain in the house of God was torn in two from top to bottom. The earth shook and the rocks fell apart. Graves were opened. Bodies of many of God's people who were dead were raised" (Matthew 27:51–52 NLV).

Several miraculous things happened as Jesus took His last breath. First, it had turned very dark outside in the middle of the day. Then at the very moment that Jesus took His last breath, the curtain inside the holy temple of Jerusalem was miraculously torn in two. This curtain was a big deal because only the high priest was allowed to go behind it once a year to make a sacrifice for the sins of all the people. This happened because

God wanted people to know that Jesus is the only sacrifice ever needed. We all have access to God now because of Jesus' death for us. Then an earthquake happened and graves were opened. People who were dead came back to life! Verse 54 (NLV) says, "The captain of the soldiers and those with him who were watching Jesus, saw all the things that were happening. They saw the earth shake and they were very much afraid. They said, 'For sure, this Man was the Son of God.'"

The people who didn't believe in Jesus only moments ago saw these miracles take place and knew that Jesus was telling the truth about Himself.

Jesus, I believe You are who You say You are. You are Truth. I put all my trust in You.

THINK ABOUT IT:
How do you think the unbelievers felt when they saw these miracles and knew that Jesus was telling the truth?

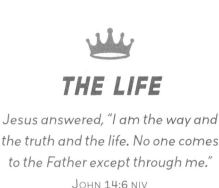

THE LIFE

Jesus answered, "I am the way and the truth and the life. No one comes to the Father except through me."

John 14:6 NIV

Pastor and Author Tim Keller wrote, "The founders of every major religion said, 'I'll show you how to find God.' Jesus said, 'I am God who has come to find you.' " There are a lot of religions in this world, but Jesus is the only way. He is the only true God.

You will learn and hear about all kinds of religions as you grow older. Many of them might sound pretty good. In fact, some of them sound quite a bit like Christianity and even call themselves Christians. But unless someone confesses Jesus Christ as Lord and commits to follow Him, the Bible tells us that person cannot go to be with God. No one gets to God the Father unless they go through Jesus Christ alone. Nothing else saves you. Working hard to be good doesn't save you. Being a truthful person doesn't save you. Being as nice as you can be doesn't save you. Going to church doesn't save you. Saying your family is Christian doesn't save you. Belonging to a Christian church doesn't save you. Being baptized doesn't save you. Only Jesus saves.

It's a heart thing. Jesus knows your heart. He

knows if what you're saying with your mouth is true. He is the only One able to look inside of you and know what's really happening.

Acts 4:12 (NIV) tells us, "Salvation is found in no one else, for there is no other name under heaven given to mankind by which we must be saved." Remember that Jesus is all the fullness of God in human form (Colossians 2:9), and He is the image of the invisible God (Colossians 1:15). Jesus is how we can see God (John 1:18).

God Himself came down to find you through Jesus. He is the way, the truth, and the life.

Jesus, I believe that You are the one true God. Through You alone, I find eternal life.

THINK ABOUT IT:

Take a look inside your heart with Jesus. Invite Him to look inside. Does He see anything that you need to talk about with Him?

THE DELIVERER

And in this way all Israel will be saved. As it is written: "The deliverer will come from Zion; he will turn godlessness away from Jacob."

ROMANS 11:26 NIV

Jesus is our Deliverer. What do you think that means? It's another way of saying that Jesus is our rescuer. Take a look at 2 Samuel 22:1–3 (NIV): "David sang to the LORD the words of this song when the LORD delivered him from the hand of all his enemies and from the hand of Saul. He said: 'The LORD is my rock, my fortress and my deliverer; my God is my rock, in whom I take refuge, my shield and the horn of my salvation. He is my stronghold, my refuge and my savior—from violent people you save me.' "

David sang to God after God delivered, or rescued, him from his enemies. Recently while on vacation, we watched a group of potential lifeguards go through training. A person pretended to be drowning in the pool and the lifeguard-in-training had to jump in and rescue that person. If they rescued the person according to the guidelines they had been taught, the trainee passed the test and became a lifeguard.

Jesus rescues us from a lot of situations, if we let Him. But unlike the lifeguards who rescue the drowning victim, Jesus carries us to a safe place and then continues to carry us for the rest of our lives. Once we've called out to Him, He will never put us down to recuperate, or get better, on our own.

Have you ever heard anyone say the Lord's Prayer? It goes like this:

"This, then, is how you should pray: 'Our Father in heaven, hallowed be your name, your kingdom come, your will be done, on earth as it is in heaven. . . . And lead us not into temptation, but deliver us from the evil one' " (Matthew 6:9–10, 13 NIV).

Jesus Himself tells us to pray and ask God to "deliver us from the evil one." That means it's important to ask God to rescue us and keep us away from evil and bad things.

Jesus, please rescue me from evil and help me run far away from bad choices.

THINK ABOUT IT:
How do you need Jesus to
rescue or deliver you today?

OUR PEACE

For He Himself is our peace, who has made both one, and has broken down the middle wall of separation.

EPHESIANS 2:14 NKJV

J esus Himself is our peace. The word "Himself" is a very important one to take note of in this scripture verse.

Think about a really difficult day you've had. What went wrong? How did you feel? Did everything feel chaotic and bad? Would it have been super easy to stop all of those feelings and make yourself feel happy in the moment? The answer is probably no, right? The Bible tells us that Jesus Himself is our peace. That means we don't have to dig down deep into our own feelings and find some peace to make a situation better again. Nope! Peace is a supernatural fruit of the Spirit that Jesus Himself brings us.

Galatians 5:22–23 (NLT) says, "The Holy Spirit produces this kind of fruit in our lives: love, joy, peace, patience, kindness, goodness, faithfulness, gentleness, and self-control."

Jesus Himself produces the fruit of peace in us (and all the other spiritual fruits) by His Spirit who is alive in our hearts!

Do you remember the story of Jesus calming the sea in the middle of a big storm? The disciples were terrified that they were going to die. They were totally freaking out! But Jesus was sleeping peacefully in the middle of the storm. The disciples frantically woke Jesus up. Take a look at what happened: "And he awoke and rebuked the wind and said to the sea, 'Peace! Be still!' And the wind ceased, and there was a great calm" (Mark 4:39 ESV).

The next time you feel like things are out of control and you are starting to freak out, pray in the name of Jesus! "Peace! Be still!" And watch as Jesus Himself brings the supernatural fruit of peace in His presence.

Jesus, I feel relieved that I don't have to dig down into my feelings to find peace by myself! You are my peace! Thanks for being with me.

THINK ABOUT IT:
How fruity are you? What fruits of the Spirit do you need to ask Jesus Himself to plant and grow in you?

CREATOR OF ALL THINGS

For in him all things were created: things in heaven and on earth, visible and invisible, whether thrones or powers or rulers or authorities; all things have been created through him and for him.

COLOSSIANS 1:16 NIV

As we've learned already, Jesus created everything! *The Message* puts it this way: "We look at this Son and see the God who cannot be seen. We look at this Son and see God's original purpose in everything created. For everything, absolutely everything, above and below, visible and invisible, rank after rank after rank of angels—*everything* got started in him and finds its purpose in him" (Colossians 1:15–16 MSG). Let's focus on one part of this scripture: "Everything got started in him and finds its purpose in him."

Jesus is your Creator. What do you think your purpose is as God's son or daughter? Here are a few scriptures that help us understand our purpose and why God created us:

> ▶ "Now this is eternal life: that they know you, the only true God, and Jesus Christ, whom you have sent" (John 17:3 NIV).

> ▶ "We know how much God loves us, and we have put our trust in his love. God is love, and all who live in love live in God, and God lives in them" (1 John 4:16 NLT).

> ▶ "Jesus replied, 'You must love the LORD your God with all your heart, all your soul,

140

and all your mind.' This is the first and greatest commandment. A second is equally important: 'Love your neighbor as yourself' " (Matthew 22:37–39 NLT).

▶ "But you are a chosen people, a royal priesthood, a holy nation, God's special possession, that you may declare the praises of him who called you out of darkness into his wonderful light" (1 Peter 2:9 NIV).

▶ "He creates each of us by Christ Jesus to join him in the work he does, the good work he has gotten ready for us to do" (Ephesians 2:10 MSG).

Jesus created us so we could know Him, love Him, love others, praise Him, and work with Him.

Jesus, thank You for making me and giving me a purpose. I invite Your Spirit to teach me all of these things.

THINK ABOUT IT:
What gifts and special abilities has God given you? How do you think God wants to use those to accomplish His purpose in your life?

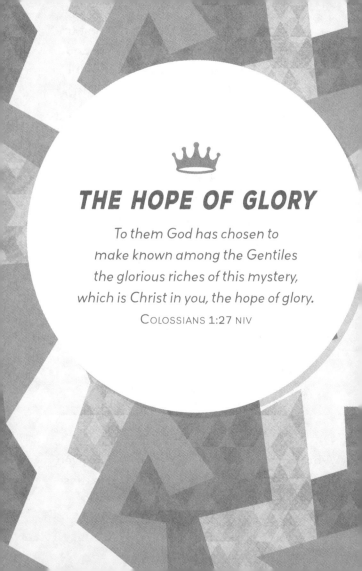

THE HOPE OF GLORY

*To them God has chosen to
make known among the Gentiles
the glorious riches of this mystery,
which is Christ in you, the hope of glory.*

COLOSSIANS 1:27 NIV

id you know that Jesus prays for you? John 17 is the prayer that Jesus prayed for Himself, for His disciples, and for us. Yes, Jesus was praying for *you*! Take a look: "I have made Your name known to them and will make it known. So then the love You have for Me may be in them and I may be in them" (John 17:26 NLV).

Jesus prayed that the same love that God the Father has for His Son, Jesus, would be in you. Isn't that amazing? Jesus' disciples didn't understand that when Jesus went back to heaven, He would send His Spirit to live in our hearts. They didn't understand that Jesus Himself would be alive in us. It is a miraculous mystery, but the Bible tells us it's true.

When Jesus was here on earth, He had limits because He was in a human body. He couldn't be everywhere at the same time. Now that He has risen and conquered death, the Spirit of Jesus Himself can be everywhere at once—even inside of you!

Having Jesus alive inside of us is our only hope for the future. If you've accepted Jesus as your

Savior, His Spirit is alive in you, teaching you all things. Isaiah 54:13 (NIV) says, "All your children will be taught by the LORD, and great will be their peace."

Jesus has all authority and power over all things. Why is this important for you? It means that you can go to Jesus with all your questions. It means that He has authority over everything that might come your way in this life. It means that He is bigger than all of your problems, failures, and fears. And you have access to this power at every moment because He is *alive in you*!

Jesus, thank You for praying for me! I'm amazed at how much You love me. Let Your Spirit come alive inside my heart so I can live for You.

THINK ABOUT IT:
Does the power to love and serve Jesus come from inside of us? Why or why not?

AUTHOR OF
ETERNAL SALVATION

And having been perfected,
He became the author of eternal
salvation to all who obey Him.

HEBREWS 5:9 NKJV

▌n John 10:18 (NLV) Jesus said, "No one takes my life from Me. I give it by Myself. I have the right and the power to take it back again. My Father has given Me this right and power."

Jesus said that He wasn't a victim. (A *victim* is a person who suffers from something bad done to them.) While people did do a lot of bad things to Jesus, He allowed it. He could've stopped it at any moment because He is the Creator of the universe. Why did He do this? Because He is the Author of Eternal Salvation. He allowed all the bad things to happen to fulfill God's purpose and to save us from our sins. There was no other way to save us and make us right with God.

Romans 6:23 (ICB) explains, "The payment for sin is death. But God gives us the free gift of life forever in Christ Jesus our Lord." We've been given the free gift of life forever—eternal salvation.

After Jesus paid for our sins, He came back alive! This is historical fact. Jesus appeared many times to many people over a forty-day period after He died on the cross and before He went back to heaven. People saw Him die and they saw Him after He came back to life! Jesus was alive! He proved that He was the Son of God and everything He claimed came true.

The same power that rose Jesus from the dead is the power that is offered to each of us who believe. Jesus has proven that He can conquer death and that death on this earth is not the end. We have the promise of eternal life in resurrected bodies with Jesus.

Jesus, I'm so thankful You died to give
me eternal life. I can't imagine the pain
You went through on purpose for me.
Help me live my life to say thanks to You!

THINK ABOUT IT:
Why does God want us to obey Him?

A REWARDER

It is impossible to please God without faith. Anyone who wants to come to him must believe that God exists and that he rewards those who sincerely seek him.

HEBREWS 11:6 NLT

Luke 18:1 (NLT) tells us, "One day Jesus told his disciples a story to show that they should always pray and never give up." Jesus went on to tell them about a widow who was seeking justice in a situation where she was wronged. The judge ignored her. But she kept coming back to him over and over until he finally listened and acted on her behalf because he was tired of being pestered by her.

This widow wasn't going to give up, and she was rewarded for that. Quitters give up because they've run out of their own strength. They have nothing left to give, so they give up in defeat. But as followers of Jesus, we depend on His strength to help us in our weakness. We trust that He hears our prayers, and unlike the judge in this story, He is never annoyed by us! He actually rewards us for coming back to Him over and over.

The power of Jesus shines through in our weakness. Allow Him to be your strength. Invite Him to give you power through His Spirit who is alive in you.

Galatians 6:8–9 (NLT) says, "Those who live only

to satisfy their own sinful nature will harvest decay and death from that sinful nature. But those who live to please the Spirit will harvest everlasting life from the Spirit. So let's not get tired of doing what is good. At just the right time we will reap a harvest of blessing if we don't give up."

Keep coming back to God every day in prayer. Be persistent. Don't give up. Jesus is your rewarder!

Jesus, just like the persistent widow, help me to always pray and never give up. Thank You that I don't have to depend on my own strength. I'd much rather count on Yours instead. Thank You for seeing me and rewarding me for coming to You!

THINK ABOUT IT:
What do you think it means to "live to please the Spirit"? What are some ways you can do that?

MY HELPER

*So we can say with confidence,
"The Lord is my helper, so I will have no
fear. What can mere people do to me?"*

HEBREWS 13:6 NLT

*J*esus is our Helper. This is a special truth to carry with you for now and always. Anytime you are in need of any help, call out to Jesus! As a child of the King, you have the Spirit of God alive inside you, helping you always. Take a look at these verses:

> ▶ "Likewise the Spirit helps us in our weakness. For we do not know what to pray for as we ought, but the Spirit himself intercedes for us with groanings too deep for words" (Romans 8:26 ESV).

> ▶ "But the Helper, the Holy Spirit, whom the Father will send in my name, he will teach you all things and bring to your remembrance all that I have said to you" (John 14:26 ESV).

There is a book for grown-ups called *When People Are Big and God Is Small*. Why do you think someone would write a book like that? What do you think it would be about?

Here's the thing: When people grow up and lose sight of Jesus as their Helper, they look to other things and people for help instead. Be cautious of this as you grow! This is one of the reasons Jesus says that the faith of a child is so important (Mark 10:13–16)! When you stay close to Jesus, He becomes your Helper for life. The faith you have right now is *so* important—it can change your whole future!

But when you put your focus on other people and things, God can become small and unimportant to you. And suddenly people and their problems become more important than your faith. It will be really hard to receive help from Jesus when your faith in Him is small. It's not because He moved, but because you did.

Jesus, thank You for being my Helper and Guide. Please help me to keep my eyes and my heart set on You throughout my lifetime.

THINK ABOUT IT:
If you felt yourself moving away from Jesus your Helper, what could you do to get close to Him again?

THE TRUE GOD

*We know also that the Son of God has come
and has given us understanding, so that we
may know him who is true. And we are in him
who is true by being in his Son Jesus Christ.
He is the true God and eternal life.*

1 JOHN 5:20 NIV

The Bible makes it clear that God has made Himself known to us through His creation. Signs of God are everywhere. Miracles are everywhere. We are without excuse when it comes to believing that intelligent design is behind every natural wonder.

Check out Romans 1:19–20 (MSG): "But the basic reality of God is plain enough. Open your eyes and there it is! By taking a long and thoughtful look at what God has created, people have always been able to see what their eyes as such can't see: eternal power, for instance, and the mystery of his divine being. So nobody has a good excuse."

Do you know what an *atheist* is? It is someone who does not believe there is a God. One former atheist named Lee Strobel said that he didn't become a Christian because he thought God would make sure he'd have a happier life. He said it was because the evidence for Christ was so strong. Lee couldn't disprove that Jesus was the Son of God and that He rose from the dead. And so, given the proof, becoming a Christian seemed the only thing that made sense to Lee.

Jesus Christ is the one true God. He proved it by coming alive after He was put to death. Everything He ever said was and is true. Isaiah 42:5–6 (NLT) says, "God, the LORD, created the heavens and stretched them out. He created the earth and everything in it. He gives breath to everyone, life to everyone who walks the earth. And it is he who says, 'I, the LORD, have called you to demonstrate my righteousness. I will take you by the hand and guard you, and I will give you to my people, Israel, as a symbol of my covenant with them. And you will be a light to guide the nations.'"

Jesus, my one true God, I'm amazed that You want to take me by the hand and guide me. Thank You for Your love for me.

THINK ABOUT IT:

Can you picture the God of the whole universe holding your hand? Can you draw a picture of what you see?

THE ALPHA AND OMEGA

"I am the Alpha and the Omega,"
says the Lord God, "who is, and who
was, and who is to come, the Almighty."

REVELATION 1:8 NIV

What are the first and last letters of our alphabet? A and Z, right? Well, the first letter of the Greek alphabet is called Alpha. Guess what the last letter of the Greek alphabet is called?

Did you guess Omega? Then you're right. Jesus is the Alpha and Omega. He says He is the first and the last, the beginning and the end. Hebrews 13:8 (NLT) tells us, "Jesus Christ is the same yesterday, today, and forever." He is full of love, grace, and truth—and He never changes.

Did you know that Jesus is coming again one day? Take a look at what Jesus says about what is happening right now:

> *"Don't let your hearts be troubled. Trust in God, and trust also in me. There is more than enough room in my Father's home. If this were not so, would I have told you that I am going to prepare a place for you? When everything is ready, I will come and get you, so that you will always be with me where I am. And you know the way to where I am going." (John 14:1–4 NLT)*

Right now, Jesus is preparing a place for you in His Father's house. How amazing is that? When everything is ready, He will come back for all of us who love Him. So what are we supposed to do in the meantime? Love God and love others. In Luke 12:40 (NIV) Jesus tells us, "You also must be ready, because the Son of Man will come at an hour when you do not expect him."

Jesus could return at any moment. And guess what happens then? Take a look in your Bible at Revelation 21:1–4. Here's a sneak peek: " 'He will wipe every tear from their eyes. There will be no more death' or mourning or crying or pain..." (v. 4 NIV).

Jesus, thank You for the perfect plans
You have for my life. I'm so grateful
that I get to be with You forever!

THINK ABOUT IT:
What would you like your room to look like in your Father's house?

THE ALMIGHTY

"I am the Alpha and the Omega—the beginning and the end," says the Lord God. "I am the one who is, who always was, and who is still to come—the Almighty One."

REVELATION 1:8 NLT

Dictionary.com defines *almighty* this way: "having unlimited power; omnipotent, as God." God calls Himself Almighty in Genesis when He is talking to Abram (Abraham). Then all through the Bible we see God being called "the Almighty." His power has no end. He is greater than all other beings. When we call God the "Almighty," we are declaring His greatness and calling on His power.

Here are some great verses to pray and praise God:

▶ "Who is he, this King of glory? The LORD Almighty—he is the King of glory" (Psalm 24:10 NIV).

▶ "Restore us, God Almighty; make your face shine on us, that we may be saved" (Psalm 80:7 NIV).

▶ "LORD Almighty, blessed is the one who trusts in you" (Psalm 84:12 NIV).

▶ "Who is like you, LORD God Almighty? You, LORD, are mighty, and your faithfulness surrounds you" (Psalm 89:8 NIV).

▶ "Whoever dwells in the shelter of the Most High will rest in the shadow of the Almighty" (Psalm 91:1 NIV).

▶ "Holy, holy, holy is the Lᴏʀᴅ Almighty; the whole earth is full of his glory" (Isaiah 6:3 ɴɪᴠ).

▶ "I will be a Father to you, and you will be my sons and daughters, says the Lord Almighty" (2 Corinthians 6:18 ɴɪᴠ).

▶ "We give thanks to you, Lord God Almighty, the One who is and who was, because you have taken your great power and have begun to reign" (Revelation 11:17 ɴɪᴠ).

Take some time in prayer right now. Read through each verse. Ask Jesus what He wants to show you. What is He saying to your heart through these scriptures?

Jesus, You are God Almighty. You are all-powerful and You can do anything! I believe this is true. I'm so thankful You care about me. Show me who You are and help me know You more and more.

THINK ABOUT IT:
Which one of these verses
speaks the most to you?

THE MORNING STAR

"Here's the reward I have for every conqueror, everyone who keeps at it, refusing to give up: You'll rule the nations, your Shepherd-King rule as firm as an iron staff, their resistance fragile as clay pots. This was the gift my Father gave me; I pass it along to you— and with it, the Morning Star!"

Revelation 2:28 MSG

J esus is called the Morning Star several places in the Bible:

> ▶ "I, Jesus, have sent my angel to give you this message for the churches. I am both the source of David and the heir to his throne. I am the bright morning star" (Revelation 22:16 NLT).

> ▶ "We also have the prophetic message as something completely reliable, and you will do well to pay attention to it, as to a light shining in a dark place, until the day dawns and the morning star rises in your hearts" (2 Peter 1:19 NIV).

When you get a little bit older, you might watch an epic movie series called the Lord of the Rings. There are some pretty scary parts in it, so don't ever watch it without your parents' permission. It is based off a classic book series by J. R. R. Tolkien. In the movie, a young man named Frodo sets off on a very dangerous journey to make right something that was very wrong. He faces a lot of difficult challenges that drain him of all his strength. He meets some helpers along the way. One of the helpers is a powerful character who gives Frodo a special necklace. It glows in the dark specifically when all other lights go out. Frodo uses it when he is being attacked in the darkness by something very scary. The light forces the monster to leave.

Jesus is our special light that glows in the darkness when all other lights go out. His name is all-powerful, and when He is present, the darkness must flee. You can trust that when you are in a dark and scary place, Jesus will bring the light of His presence when you call on Him for help.

First John 1:5 (NLT) says, "This is the message we heard from Jesus and now declare to you: God is light, and there is no darkness in him at all."

Jesus, You are my light. I trust You to light up the darkness when I'm afraid.

THINK ABOUT IT:

Where do you need the light of Jesus right now?

THE AMEN

"To the angel of the church in Laodicea write: These are the words of the Amen, the faithful and true witness, the ruler of God's creation."

REVELATION 3:14 NIV

Do you know what *amen* means? We hear it often enough—we even say it after every prayer. But have you ever wondered what it actually means?

It is most commonly used to mean "so be it," or "may it be so." You are basically stating your agreement with something. You agree that what you are hearing is "faithful and true."

There are several powerful prayers from the Bible where we see this:

> ▶ "Now may the God of peace, who through the blood of the eternal covenant brought back from the dead our Lord Jesus, that great Shepherd of the sheep, equip you with everything good for doing his will, and may he work in us what is pleasing to him, through Jesus Christ, to whom be glory for ever and ever. Amen" (Hebrews 13:20–21 NIV).

> ▶ "If anyone speaks, they should do so as one who speaks the very words of God. If anyone serves, they should do so with the strength God provides, so that in all things God may be praised through Jesus

Christ. To him be the glory and the power for ever and ever. Amen" (1 Peter 4:11 NIV).

Amen! So be it! Those words are powerful and true.

But the Bible also tells us that Jesus Himself is the Amen! What could that possibly mean? Take a look at this little but very powerful and important verse right here: "All the promises of God find their Yes in him. That is why it is through him that we utter our Amen to God for his glory" (2 Corinthians 1:20 ESV).

Author and pastor John Piper has said that when you know that *Amen* and *Yes* have the same meaning, then this verse from Corinthians makes even more sense. . . . Basically, God says yes through His promises...and we say yes to Him when we pray.

Jesus, You are faithful and true. God says yes to me because of You! I'm so thankful. Amen!

THINK ABOUT IT:

What is Jesus saying yes to you about?
Write a special prayer to Jesus about this.

If you enjoyed
Wonderful Names of Jesus,
you'll also enjoy this sneak peek into
180 Prayers to Change the World for Kids,
also available from Barbour Publishing.

YOU CAN MAKE A DIFFERENCE.

Sure, you're just a kid, but you can still change the world around you. Think about those words for a moment. No matter where you come from, where you live, what school you go to, or what grade you're in, God can use you to make a difference for eternity. Whether you have red hair and freckles, blue eyes or brown, you can stir things up (in a good way!) in the lives of those around you. God wants to use you. Yes, *you*, the kid with the peanut butter on your face and mismatched socks on your feet. Isn't that cool? He says you're a world changer. Don't you love that? It's time to start seeing yourself as someone who can bring change to the world, kiddo. That's why this book was written: to help you pray. Check it out! Every day you'll find a new topic, a prayer, a scripture, and a "be the change" activity—something you can do to grow in your faith or to help others. (Note: some activities might require help from a grown-up!) Nothing can hold you back when you start to see yourself as a world changer. What are you waiting for? Let's go!

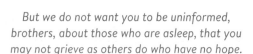

RANDOM ACTS OF KINDNESS

But we do not want you to be uninformed,
brothers, about those who are asleep, that you
may not grieve as others do who have no hope.

1 THESSALONIANS 4:13 ESV

Random acts of kindness. They're so fun, Lord! I love dreaming up all sorts of ideas—things I can do to bless kids, grown-ups, friends, family members, or even strangers. Coaches, teachers, the clerk at the supermarket. . .I want to bless them all with unexpected encouragement and surprises. Elderly neighbors, co-workers, expectant moms. . .they all need Your touch and a reminder that they are not alone. I need Your help to come up with creative ideas. What a great time we're going to have—You and me—dreaming up cool things to let these amazing people know You haven't forgotten them. Let's get started, Lord! Amen.

BE THE CHANGE
Surprise a stranger by complimenting them.

IN THE SAME WAY

In the same way, let your light shine before others,
so that they may see your good works and give
glory to your Father who is in heaven.

MATTHEW 5:16 ESV

Lord, I know the only chance I have of making a real difference in this world is to follow the example of Your Son, Jesus. He stepped *w-a-y* outside of His comfort zone and approached people in practical ways. If they needed food, He made sure they had food. Yum! If they needed healing, He healed them. Amazing! Best of all, He took the time to get to know each person, to check out their needs before fixing their problem. That way, they truly felt cared for. Today, please point out some-one I can help, a person who needs a little light in his or her life. I want to get to know that person, Lord. Maybe they need a friend like me. I want to be the hands and feet of Jesus to someone in need, I pray. Amen.

....

BE THE CHANGE

Give in a sacrificial way, as Jesus did,
and offer to clean out your parents' garage or attic.

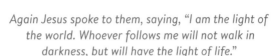

WORLD CHANGERS

Again Jesus spoke to them, saying, "I am the light of the world. Whoever follows me will not walk in darkness, but will have the light of life."

JOHN 8:12 ESV

I've been reading Bible stories of the lives You changed—Abram, Moses, David, Rahab, Jonah and so many more. Whew! There's quite a list of world changers in there! Not all of these people were willing at first. I can't blame them for being scaredy-cats! I get a little nervous myself. But here's the cool part: You used every one of these people to change the world. They made a big difference in the lives of others wherever they went. I want to be like that, Lord! Today I choose to give up my fear (Oh, help!) and to look for those who are in need. Give me Your ears to hear and Your eyes to see. I want to shine brightly, Lord, but not in my own strength. May I never forget—You're the leader, Jesus. I'm the follower. Amen.

....

BE THE CHANGE
Ask a parent to take you to a local soup kitchen to volunteer. You might just make a few friends along the way.

PAY IT FORWARD

God saw that the light was good.
He divided the light from darkness.
GENESIS 1:4 NLV

One of the things I love most about You, Lord, is that You always pay it forward. You bless me knowing I will want to bless others. How fun! It's like a little game we play. I come up with fun and random ideas to surprise people (just to bring a smile to their faces). They get excited and pay it forward by blessing someone else. I love this game! It's the gift that keeps on giving! Show me how to pay it forward every single day, in little ways and in big ones too. I want my life to be filled with adventure, every day filled with opportunities to bless others and share Your light as I go along. This is so exciting, Lord! I'm grateful to be used by You. Amen.

....

BE THE CHANGE
Pay it forward—do a good deed for someone that
encourages them to pass it along.

YOUR BEST GIFT

Light in a messenger's eyes brings joy to the heart,
and good news gives health to the bones.

PROVERBS 15:30 NIV

I don't always feel like I have a lot to give, Lord. I don't have a lot of money, after all! Sometimes I even get a little sad thinking about this. I'm just a kid, but I want to do big things. Then I remember. . .You're not limited by money. There are a zillion ways I can impact the lives of those around me without spending a penny. I can send encouraging notes, offer to mow someone's lawn, even bless an elderly neighbor with the gift of a visit and some cookies. Today, please show me some creative, inexpensive ways I can reach out to my neighbors, my friends, elderly loved ones, and those in need. I can't wait to grab a pen and paper to make my list! Amen.

....

BE THE CHANGE
Visit with an elderly neighbor and ask them about their life.